Creating Community:
101 Ideas and Activities for the Classroom

Author

Danielle Parker

Creative Director

Rachel Lawrence

FingerPark Productions™

Teachers today, more than ever, are not just teachers. They are leaders, coaches, counselors, friends, shoulders to cry on, hands to help, ears to lend.

While the demands of education continue to grow and there never seems to be enough time, there is help to be found.

Creating Community: 101 Ideas and Activities for the Classroom is intended to help create and build a community of learners that honors individuality, voice, and togetherness for both students and teachers.

All the ideas and activities are stored in one place, so there is no more need for frantic searching or trying to remember what worked "that one time."

You are encouraged to do what works best for you and your teaching style. Encourage modifications, alterations, and adjustments.

Encourage laughter, enjoyment, and fun. All of the activities in this book are intended to work across varying ages and grades because they are adaptable, just like teaching.

This book is committed to helping both teachers and students create classroom, community, culture, and fun—August through June.

Creating Beginnings

The following ideas and activities are for beginnings—creating new memories and new goals with new people in new spaces. These can be done at the beginning of the school year, unit, or semester—any time a fresh start is desired.

1

The Name Game

With so many students to remember at the beginning of the school year, this game is a quick and entertaining way to help everyone remember names.

- Each day, pick a reasonable number, say five, and have a student volunteer aim to name five other students. Challenge several students to participate.
- As the days progress, increase the number of names.
- Candy or a prize is recommended for volunteers.
- Suggest that students use the open-hand gesture (all hands open, pointing) as opposed to one-finger pointing.

2

Alliteration Name Game

Have students form an alliteration using a positive adjective to describe themselves, such as Awesome Allison or Cool Carl.

- Have all students share their name alliterations, either verbally or with a name tent.
- Try to use the name alliterations when calling on students throughout the week.
- Try to have students use the alliterations when addressing their classmates.
- As time progresses, consider expanding the alliteration to more than one word—for example, Always Awesome Activist Allison, Caring Cool Carl.

3

Who's There? Guessing Game

Here's an engaging and active way to get students to learn names by playing a guessing game. You will need a large sheet or a blanket and should preferably be outside.

- Divide the students into two groups.
- Have two students, one from each group, volunteer to help hold up the sheet.
- The sheet must touch the ground so there's no peeking.
- Have one person from each team go up to the sheet. Make sure this person is unseen by the other team.
- On your count, or on the count of three, have the sheet-holders lower the sheet.
- Players at the sheet say their opponent's name.
- Whoever says the name of the opponent fastest wins a point for their team.
- No cheating, no helping, no peeking!

4

The Survey

An excellent way to get to know your students, and for your students to get to know one another, is to create a student survey. You can give the survey at the beginning of the school year, every quarter, when you have a new student, or whenever you feel a need to check in.

- Have students create questions.
- Let students have time to read and review the answers of their peers.
- Consider creating and reviewing the survey electronically.
- Students can complete a teacher version and a student-to-student version.

5

Categories

Learn about shared similarities by having students arrange themselves by categories. Call out (and visually display using a projector or piece of paper) one category at a time. Students must arrange themselves to find others with the same answer for that category.

- Some sample categories:
  - Birth month
  - Age
  - Favorite color
  - Favorite food
- Each time a category is formed, go around the room and have students in that category reveal their answers.

6

The Whip-Around

The whip-around is a great way to hear everyone's voice. The questions asked can have a short response or be longer and more in depth. To get students used to this activity, start with simple questions, such as "How are you feeling?" or "How was your weekend?" As always, model first.

- Can be done at the beginning of class to get students talking
- Can be done throughout the lesson or whenever you need to hear more student voices

7

The Wave

Like the whip-around, the wave is a physical display of understanding. Initially, you should be the only one to start the wave. As time progresses, allow a student to begin the wave.

- Initiate it with key vocabulary or ideas.
- Or have a student in charge of leading the wave upon your signal.

8

The Artifact

Celebrate and share a physical representation of your students. Have students bring in an artifact: something that represents them or something that was once (or still is) important to them.

- You can spend an hour or a day (or two!) briefly discussing each student's artifact.
- Or have students bring in artifacts on a certain day
- Or have students bring their artifacts in and leave them on display in the room.

9

My Other Half

On notecards, write halves of different pairs, such as "peanut butter" and "jelly." Mix up the cards and give one to each student.

- Each student must find the person holding the other half of their pair, who will be their partner for the day/week/month.
- Do this as many times as needed until students have worked with various peers.
- Examples of pairs: Marge and Homer Simpson, peanut butter and jelly, sun and moon, etc.
- Have students return the notecards and repeat as necessary.

10

Question of the Day

This is a fun activity that could work a number of ways. Have questions in a bowl ("Would you rather...?" "What would you do if...?") and ask for volunteers to answer questions. You may choose to hear a select number of responses or to hear the whole class.

- You can also have a student pull and answer a question.
- Or you can have students submit several questions anonymously.
- Decide as a class how often and how many questions will be answered.

11

Name That Person

Like the question of the day, this activity requires students to write three unknown facts about themselves on a notecard. Each day, have someone pick one notecard and read the three facts. As a class, guess who the person is.

- If the class can't successfully guess the person, add their card back into the pile.
- After the class has correctly guessed the right person, allow that person a moment to elaborate on one of the facts discussed.

12

Fun Facts

Remember those Snapple facts? This activity is a little something like that. Have students research a trivia question or a fun fact.

- Make a student or a group of students responsible for providing a daily or weekly fact.
- Keep track of the facts and reflect on them as the year goes on.
- You may request that facts be specific to a particular subject, time period, region, etc.

13

Half of a Whole

Take images, cut them in half, and pass out the halves to students. Students find their other half to complete the image, then make up a story that goes with their image.

- Be sure to set parameters for storytelling.

14

"About Me" Illustrations

A great way for students to learn about one another while practicing drawing and speaking is a six-panel "about me" illustration. For this, students will need a blank piece of paper and several crayons/markers/pens.

- Have students fold their papers so they have six equal boxes (horizontally and then in thirds).
- Next, students should number each box, 1 to 6.
- Then, prompt students with a question that they can answer by drawing in the corresponding boxes, such as these example questions:
    - Box 1: City you'd like to visit
    - Box 2: Favorite food
    - Box 3: Favorite book
    - Box 4: Favorite memory as a child
    - Box 5: Where you see yourself in five years
    - Box 6: Concert of your dreams

- Once all six boxes have been illustrated, have students gather in a group and share their boxes one by one.

15

Back to Back

Teach students that communication is complex by having them sit back to back in pairs. One student is the illustrator, with a pencil and paper. One student is the explainer, with an image (unknown to the illustrator). The explainer has to describe the image to the illustrator using only shapes, lines, and measurements.

- Set a timer.
- When time is up, have the pair review their work and reflect on their communication skills.
- Repeat with roles reversed.

16

Hot Seat

This is a fast-paced, all-around fun game. You'll probably have to model it first, and that will be an excellent way for students to learn about you.

Place a chair in the front of the room, facing students. This is your hot seat.

Sit in the hot seat for a set amount of time—say, one minute. Have a student keep time. Then, allow students to ask rapid-fire questions you must answer.

- Remind students beforehand to keep the questions school- and age-appropriate.
- You may also need to remind students that if they've already asked a question, they should let others ask.
- And on the flip side, if they haven't asked a question, they should!

17

Class Goals

As a class, set goals for the week or unit, and set a collective goal. Goals should be focused around both learning and personal outcomes.

- Spend time reviewing said goals.
- Spend time reflecting on said goals and asking for help, as needed.

18

That Was Then; This is Now

You can use this catchphrase to have students compare their younger selves to now.

- Beginning of the school year? Have students think about who they were at the end of last school year.
- Or do this reflection over a longer period of time—from freshman to senior year, or from sixth to eighth grade, or from the beginning of the semester until now. We are changing, so much, so fast, all of the time.
- They can do an essay, PowerPoint, or visual (collage, illustration, etc.). Categories of change: music, food, friends, ideals, beliefs, etc.

19

Apology Accepted

We err; we are human. Find time to model, or address, the ways in which we can and should apologize in our classrooms. With your class, list who and what should be addressed in an apology, as well as how. And as the adult, you will need to model this behavior when necessary.

- Show them examples of both verbal and non-verbal apologies.
- Reinforce the importance of ownership and accountability.
- Reinforce the idea of growth and learning.

20

The Road Here

How did we get here? What roads did we take? Begin this activity by reviewing Frost's poem "The Road Less Traveled" for inspiration.

- Have students illustrate their life maps. How is it that they ended up here?
- Provide a minimum number of "stops" or events that they must describe that ultimately got them to here.
- Expand upon the road metaphor and have them plan the future road.

21

License Plate

Have students create their own custom license plates that represent and describe them.

- Use a combination of letters, numbers, and symbols for them to create unique handles.
- You can stick to the standard seven-letter combo or expand it as desired.
- Design, share, and display the plates around the room.

22

Bumper Sticker

Show students popular bumper stickers and—yep, that's right—have them design and create their own. The bumper stickers can be something serious or silly, with a personal mantra or just a fun quote.

- Have students share their bumper stickers.
- Display the bumper stickers.

23

Connected by a String

Grab some yarn and let's have fun. This is a great activity to teach students how truly connected and similar we all are. It is also a great way to get you and your students talking and moving.

- Take yarn and turn it into a ball.
- Have students arrange themselves in a circle, facing one another.
- Pose a question to the circle. Whoever has the ball must answer. After answering, that person can toss the ball to the next person.
- Every time the ball is in someone's hands, they hold on to a bit of string. Eventually, a web should be made, connecting all students.
- Another way to do this activity is to have whoever has the string ask a question and throw the ball to the person they'd like to answer it. That person then makes sure to hold on to a bit of string after they do.

- Yet another way to play is for you to pose a question, perhaps a "Raise your hand if..." and every person who agrees or can answer the statement holds and then passes a bit of the string.

24

Class Codes

Create a code of conduct that everyone agrees to live by. Have students brainstorm what makes a successful classroom and why that is important in the learning process.

Similarly, have students review what they feel is counterproductive in both teachers and peers, and compile a list.

- As a class, agree upon what is truly feasible, and create a classroom agreement for the year.
- Have students sign the agreement and review it as necessary.
- Consider sending the code home for parents to review and sign, too.
- Create a shield, crest, or image to accompany the code (can be done first individually and then voted on as a class).

For Your Notes

Creating Space

The next ideas and activities are all about the physical space you and your students inhabit. Have fun, get creative, and make something magical.

25

Quote of the Day

"With the new day come new strengths and
new thoughts."—*Eleanor Roosevelt*

Inspiring quotes can be great to have on your
board or embedded in the lesson's PowerPoint
or handouts. Have the students find one of their
favorite quotes. Collect all quotes in a jar or
basket, and ta-da—a plethora of quotes from the
students.

- Consider letting students use song lyrics
  or poetry.
- Present both the quote and the student
  who submitted the quote. This student
  could even spend a moment discussing
  how they found said quote and why they
  find it relevant.
- Compile the quotes and use them to help
  reflect at the end of the year. Review the
  ones that resonated the most, and
  discuss why.

26

This Day in History

Have students sign up to research and present a fun factoid about their day in history.

- Consider assigning days to students by birthday month.
- If doing this activity daily is too hard, you can modify the exercise so students are presenting on a week or month.

27

Seating Arrangements

The seating chart game: When to do it, how often, and why? Big questions. Every now and again, consider switching up seating.

- Seat by birthday, by favorite color, by age, or by the one person a student absolutely needs to sit next to.
- Change up the seats often for fun!
- Allow student choice when classroom dynamics merit it.

28

The Great Wall

The great wall of...poetry? Quotes? Musicians? Math problems? Consider dedicating wall space in your room and making it a "great wall."

- Allow students time to add to the wall by finding poetry they love, by adding their favorite inspirational sayings, or by posting a positive pick-me-up.
- Allow students time to admire the wall.
- Change the wall as often as necessary.

29

Bulletin Board

A student-run classroom bulletin board is great for announcements, reminders, and celebrations. Consider one large bulletin board for all your classes or, if you teach multiple sections, several small ones. Up to you!

30

Photo Gallery

With all the great photo technology that exists, a classroom photo gallery is a great way to decorate the space. Polaroids and their friends are all back in style. You could even use your cellphone to take and print photos.

- Take photos on the first day of school and hang them up. Return them to students on the last day.
- Take photos as a class on important occasions.
- Take photos after or during presentations or any other memorable learning activities.
- Have designated class photographers.
- Create fun backdrops for photos.

31

Baby Photo Gallery

Along the same lines as the photo gallery is one even cuter...a baby photo gallery! Ask students to bring in younger photos of themselves to put up. You can have students guess that baby, decorate according to graduating class, or just have a really cute space with really cute baby photos.

- You may also make copies of student photos so that no originals are harmed.

32

Names on the Board

"Hey, Miss, why is my name on the board?" is a question I get whenever I put a student's name on the board. In truth, it can be scary, signaling to everyone that perhaps someone has done something wrong. Turn this upside down and write the names of students you want to praise, to thank, to shout out, on the board. They'll love it, and so will you.

33

Happy Birthday to You!

So many students, so many birthdays. As a class, come to a consensus about how birthdays are celebrated. You can create or print monthly calendars and have students write their names on their birthdates.

- You can celebrate students by months or on their actual dates.
- You can celebrate students by zodiac sign.
- You can have reusable birthday hats that students wear and take photos with.
- You can do it big, or you can do it small; just decide as a group!

Creating Everyday Greatness

The next ideas and activities are intended for everyday use. They can be embedded into your daily or weekly routine however you see fit. They are great; they are fun. They take time and practice. Find out what works for you and your students, and modify and own these practices as necessary.

34

3:1

Write this ratio down. Stick a post-it on your laptop. This is the recommended ratio of positive (3) to negative (1) comments.

Sometimes, when managing hundreds of students a day, on top of all that is going on, we may forget the importance of positive talk.

Write yourself a reminder. Having an exceptionally hard day? Up the ratio—try 5:1 or even 7:1. This will help you to focus on the positive things happening, even if they are as simple as saying, "John, so happy you're here today," "Thank you for taking out your pencil," or "Thank you for being here."

35

Shout-Outs

Take a moment each class to shout out a student for any of the awesome things that they do but that may get overlooked.

- Build more community by having students shout out other students.
- Challenge: Ask to hear at least x number of shout-outs a day. This will push students to get talking and to get thanking!

36

Share Schedule

Put up a rotating schedule throughout the week for four or five students to share how they are feeling that day. This is their share day all year.

- Consider a set list of questions or guidelines that all students respond to.
- Students can clap, snap, or do something to show their appreciation for the share.

37

Star of the Week

Each week, a student is chosen to fill out a sheet with important information about them. On Monday, they present their sheet. The sheet and their picture hang up on the wall for the week.

- Keep the stars hanging in the room or on the ceiling to light up the sky!

38

Appreciation Manager(s)

Have one or two students in charge of leading class appreciations. You can appoint the same student(s) for the entire year or switch off. Students stand in front of the class at check-in time and facilitate the appreciations.

- As a class, decide on the parameters (how many, how long appointments will last, etc.) for appreciation managers.

39

Pair Shares

Get students in the habit of speaking and sharing their voices with pair (or elbow partner) shares.

- Set a timer to get students into deep discussion.
- Mix up who speaks first and who listens.
- Varying partners is always encouraged.

40

Weekend Check-Ins

Coming back from the weekend, a long weekend, or even a break, it is always nice to give students a moment to check in with themselves, the class, and you. Consider having them do brief check-ins with an elbow partner, as a class discussion, or in groups of your choosing. Then spend a moment to focus on the week ahead.

- What goals can be set?
- What needs to be done to be successful?
- Plan your work and work your plan!

41

This Makes Me Happy!

Students draw something on paper that makes them happy and share it with the class.

- Post drawings around the room.
- Have a brief discussion about said drawings (think "whip-around").
- Have time to celebrate joy!

42

The Art of the Letter

The letter, in all forms, styles, and lengths, is an important communication tool. Write letters often. Have the students write to you, you write to the students, and the students write to other students. They can even write to characters, people from the past, or people in the future.

Model great letters from people throughout history to affirm that this form is also a great art and that being able to express oneself in writing never goes out of style.

43

Letter to Students

A great way to check in with students is by writing them a good ol' fashioned letter. Write your letter, make a copy for every student, and then read your letter aloud to the students.

- Great for the beginning of the school year, after a break, or any time you may need to reset with your class.
- Type or write by hand.
- Embed questions, perhaps in bold, that you want students to answer or think about.

44

Student-to-Teacher Letters

An excellent way for students to respond is, of course, for them to write a letter back to you. Sometimes our students have a lot to say but don't or (for whatever reasons) can't. A letter gives them space to address you personally, without any fear.

- If you can, respond to their letters to you. While there will be lots of letters, there will be a great, positive return.

45

Letter to My Future Self

Sometime during the beginning of the school year, have students write letters to their future selves. These could be about goal-setting, their future, or something to remember about this date.

Have them address the envelopes; then put them someplace safe. At the end of the school year or the beginning of the next year, mail them or have the students' current teacher pass them out.

46

Student-to-Student Letters

As an extension of other letter-writing activities, allow students an opportunity to write to other students. Perhaps you want to have them do this after a presentation, or during a unit, or anytime you need students to communicate with one another.

- Make sure students are clear on the letter-writing expectations.
- They can write by hand or on an electronic platform such as Google Classroom.

47

Burned Letters

Sometimes there are things that need to be expressed for expression's sake, things that need to be said but are never heard.

For this activity, students and teacher write letters that will never be read but will instead be burned (or destroyed in an appropriate manner).

- Have students write letters to themselves, or someone else, to express their feelings.
- Have students seal the letters.
- Burn or otherwise destroy them in an appropriate manner.
- Have students reflect on what they needed to let go of and why.
- This could be done at the end of every quarter or semester as a symbolic way to restart.

48

Interviews

An engaging way to get students interacting with one another and talking is to have them practice their interviewing skills. This is a great activity at the beginning of the year or after a break (or any time, really). Students get to move around and talk to one another. After the interviews, students can share out loud. You can expand the activity to a more thorough newspaper-like interview.

- Sample questions for after a break:
  - How was your break? If you had an extra week of break, what would you do? What are your goals for the remainder of the year?
- Sample questions for the beginning of the school year:
  - What is one thing someone may not know by looking at you?
  - Describe your summer in one word.
  - What are you most looking forward to this school year?

49

Positive Phone Calls Home

You're busy. Very busy. But if you can, once a week, select several students and call their homes with a positive message. You'll have a chance to check in with their caretakers and build rapport, and all parties will be thankful to hear the good news.

50

Post-It Power

Post-its are great.

Post-its are fun.

Post-its can be used to promote positivity. Give students post-its and have them write something positive to post on their desks or on the backs of other students. Or you can write a positive note and stick it on a student's desk.

51

One-on-Ones

So many students, so little time.

When students are working independently, try to do brief one-on-one check-ins. Consider talking with five students a period, or a week. The goal is for you to eventually speak with everyone individually in a more personal way.

- Don't forget to set a timer.
- Keep a list of all the students you've checked in with.

52

Goal-Setting

As often as you can, provide space for students to think about and set personal goals. Further, provide time for them to review and modify those goals.

- If goals are met, consider ways to celebrate and give credit for what's been accomplished.
- If goals still need time to be met, what can be done to help students get to their destinations?

53

Four Corners

The four corners activity is a great way to engage students in group and class discussion.

You can label each corner of the room in various ways. For example, you might designate them as "strongly agree," "agree," "disagree," and "strongly disagree" or as "strong yes," "yes," "maybe," and "no."

Pose questions for students—either out loud or on the projector—and require students to answer by choosing a corresponding corner.

Once in the corner, the students must share their responses with their peers.

This exercise can be done with "getting to know you" questions and "would you rather" questions or with general questions. It can also be used in lessons to prompt discussion.

54

Twitter Wall

280 characters or fewer? You got it!

Teach brevity with Twitter. Students can respond to, analyze, and write their own short tweets on a Twitter timeline. Or you can provide tweets for students to analyze.

- Display responses.
- Expand upon this by creating a writing assignment to review and reflect upon student responses.

55

Tap Your Shoulder

Split students evenly into an inner circle facing in (eyes closed and stationary) and an outer circle (eyes open). Say things like "Tap the shoulder of someone who's made you laugh" or "Tap someone who is a great listener" and have students go around tapping shoulders. Switch circles and repeat.

- Consider adding a personal or class reflection after the activity.

56

Location Change

Occasionally, we all just need a little change of scenery. Be it for ten minutes or ten days, see about holding class outside, in the quad, or on the football field.

- Prepare students in advance so they know what necessary items to bring (blankets, sunglasses, even some sunscreen).
- Or keep these items in the classroom for impromptu location changes.

57

Books I'm Reading

As a teacher, you are one of many models for your students, including when it comes to reading.

When you're reading a book, print a copy of the book cover and the author information, and display both. Give the students a moment to ask questions about the book. Change the info when you begin a new book.

58

Book Exchange

Have students bring in their favorite books or any books they are willing to exchange with or lend to another student. You can also have book talks, tea over books, or student-led book clubs.

- Spend time creating and cultivating a love of reading.

59

Books We've Read

A single spark can start a flame. A single word can turn into a million. If you teach a class with heavy reading, consider tracking words read. If that doesn't seem feasible, have students track the books they've read.

As a class, keep a running log of both. Celebrate big milestones—you'll be surprised how fast the collective can get to a million words read!

- Bonus: Have students make "I've finished" signs after every book they read. Post all signs throughout the year, and watch them pile up as the reading happens!

60

Problems Solved

Just as you do with words read, keep track of problems solved or hours of learning.

- Everyone will be fascinated to see and know just how much time they've contributed to learning and growing.

61

Emojis/Memes

We are living in a digital age. There are lots of great and appropriate ways to use emojis and memes in class. Use emojis (and appropriate memes) to prompt discussion, begin check-ins, help students understand topics, and teach about context and subtext.

For a warmup, you can pick several emoji faces that students can identify to describe their weekend, their week, or any other thing.

62

Meditation

Meditation can be a wonderful tool in the classroom. It doesn't necessarily need to happen for long stretches of time (because who has those, right?), but it can be something that starts off short and builds gradually.

You can begin each class with a short meditation as a way to prepare for the day's learning.

- This is a practice that takes time but has benefits.
- Don't give up.
- It is a life-long skill that students can take with them forever.

63

Breathing Exercises

Like meditation, a quick breathing exercise can really center both your students and you. Take a big deep breath in (hold it) and exhale.

Teach students about the importance of breathing, about being able to refocus and re-center energy and thoughts, all with their breath.

- Variations: Long inhalations and exhalations
- Please make sure to research and familiarize yourself with this practice.
- Please also make sure all students are in good health and can participate.

64

Inner/Outer Circle

The inner/outer circle is a great way to provide space for discussion.

- Divide students into two groups.
- One group forms the inner circle; one group forms the outer circle.
- Both circles should be facing one another in preparation for discussion.
- Pose a question to the group.
- Have students discuss it in pairs.
- Prompt either inner or outer circle members to move x number of steps to their right or left.
- Repeat.

65

Collaborative Storytelling

Write a story, finish a story, answer a question, review a theory, or analyze a poem—together!

There are several ways this can be done. If students are in rows, the first person of the row can write for a select amount of time, then pass the paper back until everyone in the row has added on. Or the paper can be passed until every student in the class has added on to it. You can also work in table groups—just as long as the ideas and the papers are shared and passed!

66

Reflections

Provide space to be reflective.

When you can, set aside some time for reflection in a journal, a letter, or a worksheet or with a partner, then in a class discussion. Reflect at the end of the week so it becomes a practice that students are comfortable with.

Questions to ask:

- What are three things that went well this week/month/unit?
- What is one thing that needs improvement?
- Who or what are you grateful for?
- What have you learned?
- What are your hopes for next week?

67

Class Message Board

There are various internet platforms that will allow for a class message board. You can post a question and have students respond to both you and a set number of their classmates. This is an excellent way to prompt dialogue and discussion as well as to reinforce the importance of clear and effective writing.

- Don't forget you can use the message board to talk about homework, birthdays, announcements, trips, etc.

68

Show Me a Pic

Our phones are a part of our daily lives and can often be used in the classroom.

The photos on our phones can go a long way toward helping us learn about our classmates and continuing to build community.

- When you return from a break, have students share pictures of things that best represent their breaks.
- Have students take photos over the weekend to share on Monday.
- Have students become photographers, documenting their friends, family, or lives. Have them share their images with classmates.
- Remind students that all photos must be school appropriate and follow school guidelines.

69

Buddy, Buddy

Each month/quarter/semester, let students exchange information with a homework buddy.

Each member of the duo is responsible for helping the other stay accountable for and on top of any work missed.

- Check in about goals, homework, attendance.
- At the end of each time as partners, have them reflect on their work together and thank one another for time together.

70

Extra Credit

Extra credit is always a hot topic. However, think of things that can extend student learning and engagement, and offer extra credit for doing something new. Consider:

- Beach clean-up
- Volunteering
- Donations made
- Movies related to the topic
- Art galleries
- Science center or museum visits

Give students a chance to be recognized for things they do outside the classroom that help contribute to their development as young people in the world.

71

Creating the Test

Give students an opportunity to be metacognitive about their learning and create problems for a test (or quiz or exit slip).

This can be done on paper or on various online platforms. Then, students can allow others to take their tests and provide feedback!

72

Classroom Newsletter

A great way to keep in contact with parents and caretakers is to write and send a holiday or seasonal newsletter.

- Briefly update the adults in your students' lives about what has happened and what to expect next. And, if you can, add a personal line or two.
- This is a great informal way to keep in touch, and your students will remember the effort.
- Have students self-address their own envelopes before break.

Creating Fun

This is going to be fun, promise!

The next ideas and activities are intended to bring a different sound and mood to the classroom. They are enjoyable and student-approved.

73

Office Hours in the Community

Take that grading or lesson planning offsite!

Consider a local coffee shop or café, and let your students and caretakers know they can meet you there. You may also want to encourage other colleagues to join you so that students and caretakers are able to speak with more than one of you. And who knows? Maybe you'll get a coffee or two out of it!

74

Class Countdown

Who doesn't love a good countdown?

Winter break, spring break, end of the year—so much to look forward to.

- Decide, as a class, what to count down to.
- Dedicate a space to the countdown.
- Allow students to take turns physically changing the count.
- Or find an online platform that will keep track for you.

75

Class Instagram

A great way to document and remember the year is through a class Instagram account.

Each week, a different student can be in charge of documenting or updating the account.

- Have a focus.
- Reminders, homework, etc.

*Double-check your school rules and employee handbook information about social media.

76

Class Website

Similar to the class Instagram page is the class website.

- Have students be responsible for creating and curating certain sections.
- Spend time documenting the work that's being done.

*Double-check your school's rules and employee handbook with regard to social media.

77

Got Your Back

Take a moment to let students know that they are valued and appreciated with this activity. Students tape paper on their backs and walk around writing affirmations/appreciations on each other's backs.

- Set a timer.
- Words can be anonymous.
- Review and reflect after.

78

Open Mic Night

Open your classroom up in the evening for an open mic night! Have students share their work, read their poetry, display their art, or do anything of the sort.

- Invite community and family members.
- Offer extra credit.
- Document the event and upload photos or video to any class website or IG account.

79

S.W.A.G.

Stuff we all get: T-shirts. Hats. Buttons. Stickers. Think of it, design it, and have it made! Students will be happy to represent and have a class keepsake.

80

Class DJ

Ah, music in the classroom. And exactly whose music are we listening to?

Perhaps there are certain activities in your lesson that will allow for the class to listen to music. If so, consider a class DJ!

- For this, students can submit a song to a class playlist (think Spotify or any other streaming service).
- Or, if you don't have this/don't want to create it, have students write down songs and then individually choose songs to play.

81

Awards Ceremonies

Take time to celebrate the hard work of you and your students. When appropriate, plan an awards ceremony. Invite families, administrators, and staff.

Have food.

Plus, have students vote on awards for other students!

82

Trashketball

Got a trashcan? Then you've got trashketball!

A fun two-minute end-of-class activity is to ball up a piece of scratch paper and have students aim for the basket (trashket). Play with teams, play horse, play individually.

You can also buy small plastic basketball hoops and tape them to the back of the door. This is great, too!

83

One-Panel Illustration

Cartoons are a great way to teach and engage students. Review the one-panel cartoon and have students create their own.

One-panel cartoons can be a great way to teach about themes or main ideas, since students have less room and have to cover more ground.

84

Three- or Five-Panel Illustration

Like a one-panel cartoon, three or five panels allow students to expand upon their cartoon creations by adding more depth and detail to their art.

- Review popular cartoons.
- Have students create their own cartoons around the day's learning.
- Be specific in how many panels they can use to express an idea.

85

Art Time

More art? Yes, please!

Give students silent time to create art that pertains to the day's learning. Consider ten minutes of silent time for them to create. There are lots of great products out there—think paint, markers, and collages made from old newspapers.

86

Thank You

"This is a wonderful day. I've never seen it before."—*Maya Angelou*

There is always so much to be thankful and grateful for.

Take a moment to write thank-you cards.

Take a moment to practice gratitude in the classroom. Use your warm-ups, exit tickets, or pair shares to express things that you and your students are grateful for.

87

Postcards

Greetings from my favorite class!

Create postcards (old snack boxes or any light cardboard boxes can work great) to send with an update on what's going on and what learning is being done or with a general check-in.

- Students can write to their friends, family, or peers.
- Students can write to characters, authors, or companies.

88

Potlucks

The name says it all.

Community potlucks are a great way to break bread. Potlucks can be held after a unit or to celebrate birthdays or any big event.

Taking some time to enjoy one another's company over food is always a treat!

89

Mural

Have a large blank canvas? Create a class mural! Perhaps this can change each semester or as your space allows. Take photos and remember each class creation.

It can also be fun to make a mural on windows with window paint or on doors with butcher paper. Almost anything can be a canvas.

90

Field Trips

This one is self-explanatory but loads of fun! Depending on your grade level and content, aim for a day of learning outside the classroom walls.

- Go to museums, the movies, parks, or other classes/schools.

91

Silent Sustained

Silent sustained reading, writing, art, meditation...the possibilities are endless.

Start with small time increments and build up.

- Consider keeping track of minutes spent on this activity.
- Consider assigning a reflection piece upon completion of the day's silent sustained work.

92

Game Day

Chess? Checkers? X-Box? Clue? Puzzles?

Cards? Monopoly? Kahoot online?

A game day is a perfect way for students to engage with one another in a more relaxed setting. Ask colleagues or family members for games or puzzles that they wouldn't mind donating to the class. Teach students new games when appropriate. Winners get bragging rights!

93

Class Superlatives

Don't save the superlatives for the yearbook! At the end of the year unit/quarter/semester/month, whatever is feasible for you, have your class vote on chosen superlatives. The winner can take a picture and be recognized.

Record all winners and review them at the end of the year.

Some superlatives to consider:

- Most improved
- Most likely to have snacks
- Most likely to be your friend

94

Let's Dance

Sometimes you've been sitting too long, and you just need to move! To dance! To wiggle around!

Students will be shy at first, until they aren't! Even a good minute-long wiggle-around will help them relax and have some fun.

Bonus: use the music from the class playlist to get students hyped up.

- Have students teach you the latest dance move.
- Participate in the latest dance challenge.

95

Group Trivia

An engaging way to review facts or just have some fun is group trivia.

- Have students get into groups (size and group member choice up to you).
- Have each group come up with a team name.
- Then let the trivia fun begin!
- Have groups compete against one another.
- Group trivia can be used to review content, to review facts learned throughout the year, or for fun's sake.
- Winning team gets a prize...or bragging rights! :)

96

Rock-Paper-Scissors Champ

A student favorite! See who is the Rock-Paper-Scissors champ of the day. The way it works:

- All students stand up.
- On your call, they engage in quick pair games of RPS.
- The loser in each pair immediately becomes a cheerleader for the person they lost to, lining up behind the recent winner.
- The winners of the round then challenge someone nearby.
- While students play, the cheerleaders chant the names of their players.
- The process repeats until there are eventually two long lines of chanters and two people playing for the title.

97

Person of the Year

Inspired by *Time* magazine's Person of the Year issue, have students complete their own Person of the Year profile—of themselves.

- Or they can pick a classmate to do a profile piece on, or perhaps a member of their family or community who has had a significant impact on them and their lives.
- Sharing the finished product is always encouraged.

98

Human Knot

Time to go outside and connect, with an activity that is great for building teams and building communication skills.

Tell students to form a close circle. Then, have them stick their hands out and grab the hands of two different people around them (they can also do this with their eyes closed).

- Students should all be connected.
- Without unlocking hands, they have to untangle themselves from this knot.
- To unravel themselves, they can step over, under, and behind their classmates as best they can.

99

Kind Words

We all love and need them.

Type students' names on paper or notecards, and then distribute them. Students have to write kind words on the papers and give them to the classmates whose names are on them.

Teachers, too!

100

Volunteer

"We make a living by what we get, but we make a life by what we give."—*Winston Churchill*

As a class, think of events or ways to help your community. Meet up and volunteer together.

It is never too early to begin teaching students about civic engagement and community outreach.

- Consider blood drives, food drives, and beach cleanups.
- Invite family, friends, and coworkers.
- Consider extra credit.

101

Alphabet Game

And finally, teach students the importance of teamwork with this game.

- Have students form a circle, facing one other.
- Without any prompting or discussing, students aim to verbally say the alphabet.
- Each student must contribute at least once.
- If more than one student speaks at the same time, begin the alphabet again.
- Students will learn to support and rely on their classmates in order to achieve the goal.
- You can also substitute a number count for the alphabet.

54132833R00064